A Journey of Epic Proportions

Slay Some Dragons

By Laurette Lee

 **RESULTS PRESS**

Results Press
Unit 229
#180, 8601 Lincoln Blvd.
Los Angeles, California
90045

www.theresultspress.com

ISBN: 978-1-953089-04-5

First Edition

Copyright © 2021 by Laurette Lee

All rights reserved. No part of this book may be reproduced in any form without the prior writer permission from the publisher. The opinions and conclusions drawn in this book are solely those of the author. The author and publisher bear no liability in connection with the use of the ideas presented.

Table of Contents

CHAPTER ONE: MY STORY ---------- 7

CHAPTER TWO: MISSION, VISION, PURPOSE ---------- 19

CHAPTER THREE: FIND YOUR TREASURE ---------- 25

CHAPTER FOUR: HOW DO YOU MARKET? ---------- 31

CHAPTER FIVE: THE UNICORN FINDS HER TRIBE ---------- 39

CHAPTER SIX: THE HEALING JOURNEY ---------- 45

CHAPTER SEVEN: PATTERN BELIEFS ---------- 53

CHAPTER EIGHT: BULLET JOURNAL ---------- 59

CHAPTER NINE: A LITTLE CRAZY TO BE AN ENTREPRENEUR ---------- 83

CHAPTER TEN: THE LAST CHAPTER – GROWTH

   IS UNCOMFORTABLE ---------- 87

A SNEAK PEEK OF THE SECOND BOOK IN THE SERIES

   "A JOURNEY OF EPIC PROPORTIONS" ---------- 91

Chapter One: My Story

Where do you start on a journey, perhaps at the beginning? I was born in Edmonton, Alberta and grew up in a broken family with a twin sister and two older brothers. It wasn't always a broken family. In my life, I have had extreme blessings and, in a world of scarcity, many abundant moments. My first memory might have even been in the womb. I had a womb mate but, in my vision, it was just me. I was so excited to see the world, but my life was dark and had no light. A gentle voice told me no, no, no, not yet! Wait, be patient, your time will come. That was the first time I heard God in my life. He's cool!

I remember breathing and finding peace for the first time.

Fast forward to the family memory of all four of us under the age of four: Derrick, Lindsey, me, and Lorne on a bed with a big mirror on the headboard. I remember looking at Lorne and just knowing he was my big brother; he would protect me and love me just for being me. The other side was another baby. Not me but a different entity of a baby (my twin sister). I thought it was weird and special to have another me to grow up with. Well, her being her, I knew she wasn't me. I remember the peace of family and the warmth of coming from a home of love. Of the top things in my life, the thing I would never trade is family.

Second Memory: Home Adventures. My favorite and scariest place to play was not the rumpus room but the freezer room. They were right next to each other. We had a big freezer; you could probably live off of the food in it for a month if the apocalypse happened. I just remember hiding behind it a lot and trying to solve the mystery of life. I hid a lot during my

Chapter One: My Story

childhood. I liked being hidden and still watching the world around me. I am a sociologist first and foremost. I don't understand a lot about fitting into society. I was weird my entire life. Growing up, everywhere I went people told me, "You're weird." They would never explain why I was weird or what I did weirdly. They just used to say to me: "You're weird."

It's not easy feeling like you belong in this world when your awkwardness and individuality seem like a curse. The fact of the matter is, I always thought I believed in myself but, in reality, my self-esteem was bad and undeveloped. One of my favorite Bible verses growing up was about standing for something or falling for everything. The thing about deception is, well, it's so deceiving. Being comfortable does not mean growth. Life is super easy to take for granted. The safety of home, the safety of a sheltered life—we all know life is not safe.

A lot of my growing-up years involved me being shy and scared. I remember just calling out to a higher being and saying, "God, if You're real, comfort me! Love me." The call of the innocent child inside of me loved the magnificence of Christianity. God is very real and active in my life.

The search for meaning and purpose has always been at the forefront of my life. Ask, Knock, Seek, Find. I have journal entry upon journal entry of me trying to understand life and what my purpose in life is.

There were the awkward teenage years when I was learning to manage fear and surrender to the living universe of accepting myself.

The working years: I always say you work from the bottom to the top. My very first job was picking up garbage for the City of Edmonton. I made $5.23 an hour and my first ever paycheck was 35 dollars. The value of a dollar was hard work. I was only in Junior High and only stayed at that job for a summer.

In high school, grade 11, I thought it was time to adult up and get a part-time job while going to school. I was the classic A&W cashier; my friend worked there so I got the job. I sure learned about how to get over my shyness. You can't be shy when customers want to talk to you to get a cheeseburger. Three months came and went, and finals happened. I quit that job ASAP because school, education, and learning always come first.

When I graduated from grade 12, I knew education and Christianity were the keys to running my life.

Just before graduating, I got baptized – the same day as Lorne – March 11, 2001. The weird butterfly moment of getting baptized was the opposite of freedom. I remember it being an overly sad and scary moment.

I jumped into getting a Bachelor of Arts with a general study and a minor in sociology. These university years were moments of learning to live a surrendered life and trying my best. It took me four long years to get a three-year B of A. Trust me, it was hard, and I earned it.

During University I worked as a market researcher. This job is the definition of rejection, rejection, rejection. I made phone call after phone call after phone call. In order to survive all the rejections, I made a working persona—Jennifer Hawkins. She was fierce, aggressive, and didn't let anyone push her around. I was good at my job, and it helped me survive at University. All good things come to an end and the timing of Ipsos Reid closing just a month before graduation made it clear—a new adventure was afoot. At twenty-three, the question still popped up: What do I want to do for work as a career? Whoever has their life carved out before twenty-three, I am highly impressed by you.

I knew about the occupation of Employment Specialist, and the first time I ever heard about NOC codes, magic rang in my ears. I have never been super fascinated with careers but learning that there is a formula for finding a job intrigued the core center of my soul.

I did my due diligence of understanding what an Employment Specialist was, and how could I become one. NETWORKING: I talked to more than three Career Development Practitioners. Employment Specialist One: A retired bus driver that had no experience in the field but applied for the job because she knew someone. Employment Specialist Two: The University Employment Specialist. I remember saying, "How do I find a career, how do I figure it out, how do I make the right decision?"

Chapter One: My Story

His only response was: "Go on ALIS!" (Alberta Learning Information Services)

I was stunned; I was lost, confused, and looking for clear guidance. No one wants a website when they are looking for help. We all want love, truth, and compassion, especially when we as humans are lost.

I made a list of titans in the field: NorQuest, McBride, and Boyle Street all have employment specialists. My mission was to talk to all of them and find out how they did it. I knew from talking to a business employment specialist that your life is run by your values. If I was going to network with the best, I better have a solid four questions to ask each Titan in the field:

What is your average day like?
How did you do it? How did you become an employment specialist?
What are the benefits of working as an employment specialist?
Any other advice?

Let me tell you, it took me till I was 31 to be an employment specialist. I knew I wanted to be one at

Eight years of rejection, eight years of trying to figure out how to be an employment specialist.

= At this point, I would love to point out that a belief in self is a magical game-changer. =

Let us pop back into try, try, try again. Data Entry, Trucking, Dispatch, Mall Dispatch, Office Manager, Skatepark Leader, Market Researcher, youth leader, wood cutter, painting rails, and welder, to name a few. I tried a lot of jobs and failed often in my career journey. I think my total is over forty jobs in my entire life. I usually win if we play the game "How many jobs have you had?" I want to explain something. You are who you are. I believe in you as the person you were created to be. Every one of us as people is unique, special, and made just to be our epic selves.

Even though it took me 31 years to become an employment specialist, I was already an employment specialist when I was five, playing with my dolls and when I was 20, jumping jobs. Your purpose is your life; a gift you get to live even when you don't know you are living it.

My best memory growing up was playing facilitator to my stuffed toys. I knew I wanted to teach my toys, but I remember a pause and thinking to myself, How do people choose their careers? Every job I have had, I knew how to get it and I knew the techniques to manipulate the system. A good rejection goes a long way. A "No" does not stop you from giving up on your goals. The only thing a "No" means is "Next Opportunity." Be more resilient than the problem.

To Explain the format for Getting a Job:

Data Entry: Cold call to get information
Welder: Cold call to get information
Facilitator: Cold call to get the information

To explain the format for Career Development:

Career Development
Personality and Authentic Happiness
The Hidden Job Market
Labor Market Information
Resume/LinkedIn
Market Yourself
Work Search Basics
Interview Techniques
Labor Laws
Strategies for Success

Being a welder at 29 taught me a lot about what I wanted and what I did not want. Nothing like getting laid off in another industry before the age of thirty to feel like a total loser. My old friend, education, had to come into play. I wanted so badly to be an employment specialist, but I couldn't get

Chapter One: My Story

a job because I didn't have experience; I didn't have experience because I didn't have a job in the field. The circle of experience and getting the actual job to get experience was so frustrating. I knew what I wanted to be, but I couldn't physically do it. I shelved the aspiration to learn the trade and took a diploma in Career Development. Most employment specialists work in the field and their employers pay for their education. An average employment specialist takes over five years to get a diploma. No one paid for mine except my old friend Visa and a part-time job. It took me one full year to finish my Career Development Diploma. I had to get an emergency full-time job as a dispatcher for trucks to finish paying for school. I could not afford to drive and lost my car because I had to scrape and save to pay off my education.

I wish I could tell you as soon as I finished my Career Development Diploma, I got a job in the field.

NOPE. Two and a half years later I forced myself to get the energy to believe in myself. I still remember the interview. "You don't have experience in the field, so how can you be an employment specialist?" I just told her straight out, "I do have experience. I have education in the field, and I have taught many facilitations. I even volunteered and have been a strong leader in my volunteering career." The journey of my dream career did not end my career development. I want to say that again—getting your dream job does not mean you are done with career development.

I had a contract for eight months and loved every second of it. This was in a time of recession, and I helped a lot of people by teaching them the five steps of career development. One of the top executives for our contract came into sit in one of my facilitations to judge me. I rose to the occasion, and she was overly impressed by my strong business acumen and my natural ability to facilitate.

I got laid off because the work environment was so toxic. Looking back, the people I worked for abused me and treated me like I was a pariah because they as a company could not hit the targets the government set for them. I honestly did not care about the mistreatment because I loved the job and I loved finally getting my start in a field I so desperately loved. I respect the

Chapter One: My Story

company and respect the owner. I honestly wish to thank her for hiring me and letting me start in my chosen occupation. Perception makes a life lived the way you choose it to be. I am blessed and grateful for my time in that company.

When I got laid off, they give me a month before my last day. I knew I wanted to stay in the field and was tenacious in looking for a new job in my field. I'm quite sure that month I had over seven interviews and applied for over 200 jobs. At this point, I wanted to talk about rejection. To even start in my field, I am sure in a ten-year period I have had over 1,000 rejections. I would apply for the same company repeatedly. I counted the rejections for my first job in the field; it was over twelve applications to the same company and three interviews later.

It's not that I suck at interviews or that I don't know what I am doing, but when the Universe doesn't want you to succeed, it will knock you down. The thing about the Universe is at the end of the day you can control it with something called SURRENDER and belief in self. I have those key elements when I really need them. I am always my best friend.

I applied for an employment specialist job. The last Thursday I worked, I got a call for an interview the following Tuesday and got confirmation of my new second job in the industry the next day, Wednesday. I was only officially unemployed for three days. I did decide to take two weeks off at that time to have a vacation.

The job was to help people with disabilities develop their careers. I was right at home with my job, and it took me less than two weeks to be off and on my own and running the show on my contract. The boss understood that I knew my job and she trusted me to use my theories of Career Development. The contract needed 20 candidates and to find 12 of them jobs. It was an easy contract, and I easily found 18 of them successful in their chosen fields. It took a while, but we did it. Looking for a job is hard work and starting a career with a disability is a challenge. The secret is their disability always gives them a strength that surpasses their challenges. The feeling of hitting your stride in your chosen dream career is one of the best feelings in the world.

Chapter One: My Story

Life really likes to kill you. I was finding myself more and more tired every day at work.

Something was wrong with my health, but I did not know what. My life felt like it was being snuffed out. A dark peace came over my body; I was about to die. Of course, I fought back…I kept going to the doctor and saying something was wrong.

Please fight for your health if you know something is wrong. You are your best health care advocate.

My feet swelled and my doctor finally sent me for an echocardiogram. When I was sitting in the waiting room, my doctor told me to come to her clinic ASAP and go to the hospital. Once I was in the hospital a red folder was given to me stating I have CARDIOMYOPATHY and had three possible outcomes to my short 34 years of living: The outcomes were as follows:

ONE: Get worse and die. (Umm, NO)

TWO: Stay the same. I was in pretty rough shape, so that seemed like a bad option as well.

THREE: Get better. I remember telling the doctor, "I CHOOSE THE THIRD OPTION."

On the third day in the hospital, I woke up and a lot of beeping was going on around me. I remember feeling an easy peace around me. Death is easy, but it just was not my time to die. The amazing true love of my life asked me that day if I wanted anything. The one desire in my life was to have a puppy. If a person dying asks for a puppy, you have to say "Yes"—that's the rule.

Aaron had nothing to say but "Yes, of course. If you survive, you can get a puppy." (PS: We already had the best dog in the world, a little pug named Argos.)

Chapter One: My Story

Three months of disability—I lost my job after going back to work because my contract ended.

Honestly, they could have kept me on but so many factors came into play. Working with people that have disabilities and getting my own disability was so ironic and sad, all at the same time. I focused a lot that year on healing with diet and exercise.

Once I was ready to go back to work, I knew the perfect job in the industry was waiting for me. I surrendered to God and just told Him, "You got me. Find a job that pays well and lets me help people as an Employment Specialist."

The Universe answered with a five-dollar raise and the dream of working with immigrants to help them develop their careers. I helped a lot of great permanent residents settle into their careers in Canada. My only tip for immigrants coming to Canada is: Do your research, find where the companies you want to work for are before you move to a location, and always network. It's who you know; not what you know.

During my contract, my boss brought me into her office one day. It was the weirdest conversation ever. She told me I should not be working in her company because I was not an immigrant. The Canadian Labor Law rung in my ears! EQUALITY. I deeply respected my boss and I have a strong belief that equality trumps authority. I told the boss above her what had happened. I wrote up my company and wrote a formal complaint through H.R. Yes, eventually I lost my contract because of this. To be honest, I did not want to be an employment specialist anymore.

Rejection, rejection, rejection: New field: Admissions Advisor. They share a similar NOC (National Occupational Classification) code, and I just didn't want to fail in my industry anymore. It's kind of like my Rocky moment, when he gets all quiet and starts his training all over again.

I needed a win, and I needed an easy job to get ready for my comeback. I had already worked with junior high, high school, income support, people with disabilities, and immigrants. The target market I was going after was university students. I got a job at Concordia University after I applied, had

Chapter One: My Story

an interview, got rejected, and applied again. The work was the best because it was a lot of data entry and scanning. I took a good chunk of my contract to read books and think about the future.

This is where the fun happens…

All through my life, I have been a natural leader, and signs were all around me to run my own company. On my first job as an employment specialist, the best placement specialist in the company told me, "When you start your own company, I am coming with you." I thought it was weird to say because I never mentioned running my own organization, ever. On my second job in the field, everyone was so paranoid about lay-offs and contracts ending. I was never paranoid because I had a secret—I knew I was extraordinarily successful at what I do and can find a job ASAP if I needed to. By my third job in the field, I knew I would have more stability with starting my own company than relying on others to give me a paycheck.

I became unemployed on April 1, 2019 but was working under the table for a company that did career development. I wanted to know how the manager did it. How did he run his own company? I did a lot of job shadowing in specifically working right in the manager's home to see how he did it. I learned a valuable lesson about managers and business owners. If they can do it, I can do it.

I didn't feel like I was ready to start my company; I didn't want to go on E.I. (Employment Insurance). My desire was to get a four-month contract and go to Anderson Career Training Institute in the new year, 2020.

Concordia University of Edmonton was just that—a four-month contract. It let me read books like *Rich Dad, Poor Dad* (Robert T. Kiyosaki), *It Works* (R.H. Jarrett), *Rejection Proof* (Jia Jiang), *Failing Forward* (Jennifer Cohen), *Man's Search for Meaning* (Viktor Frankl), *Your Word is Your Wand* (Florence Scovel Shinn), *Surprised by Joy* (C.S. Lewis), and so many more—45 in total. Reading gives you wisdom.

I believe in myself. I am in life for the long game. Phoenix Career Development has been open for two months. Clients are coming; clients are already here. If you want to talk about your dreams and have someone with a proven track record to help your career development, please come talk to me. Laurette Lee www.phoenixcareerdevelopment.com

Be blessed. My company is a gift to yourself and magic for your soul.

Thank you, Thank you, Thank you.

Chapter Two: Mission, Vision, Purpose

How do you find your purpose? The awkward teenage years were a discovery of questions and soul-searching. Lots of yelling out to a creator/divine maker for clear understanding in life. Our journey is uncomfortable; that is how you know you're doing it right. Ignorance is bliss, but it's not helping people. Am I supposed to feel stupid? Give permission to ask difficult questions!

What is my purpose in life? What is my mission in life? What is my vision?

The Process of Self Discovery—to go through life lost is a tragedy. I felt lost for a good chunk of my childhood and my early twenties. I knew as humans we are designed for great things. I knew people were on this earth for a purpose. What was it? NO CLUE. How do you get it? ALSO, NO FREAKIN' CLUE.

Let's start with the big questions. Why are we here? Why are we created? What is our purpose? What do you want? What is your heart cry?

SWITCH TO HOPE...

The first man I had a crush on had no idea I existed. I crushed on him so bad; it was very distracting. I knew if he didn't love me back it wasn't worth all the feelings. Urgh. Feelings! I learned how to surrender and give feelings to God. Clarification is key to understanding terms. I will gladly take the rejection of a first crush to gain clarification.

I leveled up from the surrender. The story of finding your mission, vision, and purpose mirrors the adventure of a first crush. The rescue of self is the secret to finding your treasures in life. The first crush never loved me sexually. He became a brother; he became something deeper than physical.

Chapter Two: Mission, Vision, Purpose

We were meant to be in each other's life for clarification. We had a conversation one day.

Crush: "Why am I single?"

Me: "Do you understand you're a serious hottie?" Crush: NO WORDS; the feeling of confusion on his part.

Me: "I am not vying for your attention. If you liked me, you would have manned up and declared your love to me already. (We had over seven years of friendship). What kind of woman do you want? Do you want to get married? Do you want to fall in love?"

Crush: "Yes, I want to date, marry, and have children."

Me: "It's your game. Tons of women love you just for being you. Pick one and end the game of single you."

Crush: "What if…"

Me: "No what-ifs. Just fall in love, surrender. Claim your true love. You are in control; you have the power."

= Conversation over with diva Laurette getting in the last world and walking away. =

Define Terms for Clarification Sake:

Vision – "The ability to see or the ability to think about or plan the future with imagination or wisdom"

Mission – "A calling or a purpose"

Purpose – "The reason for which something is done or created, or for which one exists"

The Power of a Question:

In order to find your vision, mission, and purpose in life, you have to be willing to ask questions, be confused, and clarify. Simple questions, difficult questions—face yourself, talk to your demons, and then talk to your

Chapter Two: Mission, Vision, Purpose

light/spirit to find your moral compass. Try not to deceive yourself. Ask for wisdom. Speak to wisdom. It exists.

Ask yourself: What do I want in myself? The hardest thing you can do in life is to ask yourself, What do I want? This is my list:

Friends, trust, adventure, relationships, authenticity, best possible case scenario, making my own money, spirituality, ability to support myself, mental strength, financial health, and being leveled up, complete, whole, respected, and honored.

Here is the thing about your mission, vision, and purpose—it always exists. You have all of them without knowing it. Your purpose, vision, and mission are gifts that you can open and play with or just leave wrapped up. I want to play. Growing up, I did not play. Creative imagination was dead. I remember the day it died; it was a simple, boring day in my childhood bedroom.

The formation of my vision, mission, and purpose – I inherently knew life was about others; caring for others and living life to help support and encourage others around me. Life is long...

What kind of life would be cool to create? What is the best journey to set my life on? The vision came first. My girlfriends and I all had superhero husbands. Batman was picked first, Nightwing, Superman, and...what about me?

Best Friend: "You can have Green Lantern." Me: "What is so cool about him?"

Best Friend: "He can create anything with his power ring."

=A Long Pause= Me thinking about claiming a husband that can create anything with a power ring....

Me: "Sure, I am down with that!"

Superheroes always talk about the legendary journey. What's the definition of a legend? A well-known person with distinctive or unique characteristics

Chapter Two: Mission, Vision, Purpose

or skills. If my pretend superhero husband was legendary, I guess I should be as well.

The statement to tie it together: Epic is an adventure of a legendary journey. Fine-tune my VISION— A JOURNEY OF EPIC PROPORTIONS

I was probably in my early twenties when this was revealed to me. I searched long, and hard. The vision was always a part of me even when I didn't know it.

Purpose: The theoretical/philosophical ramification of finding a purpose is difficult. I thought my purpose was to help people. I thought my purpose was to care for others and be a good person. Seems pretty legit to me.

The death of mending from self-hate changed this purpose for me at age 34. Cardiomyopathy happened. It was rough and completely desecrated my whole outlook on life. I thought I loved myself. That concept of self-love and how deep I really hurt myself from being mean didn't actually reveal itself till that year, at 36. My purpose was too grand; it was hard to complete. The only important thing in my life was to start being happy and healthy. If I was going to die, I might as well die being happy.

Surrender again!!! The new simplicity of life.

What can I do to be happy? What can I do to be healthy?

If my life did not hit those two theories in a day, it was not worth pursuing. A purpose can change, grow, develop, and mold. It can even fly like a phoenix. The definition of a phoenix should be clarified at this time. Phoenix: "a thing that rises from the ashes with renewed youth to live through another cycle." As of this moment, my purpose is to have a happy and healthy company. Phoenix Career Development is my baby. My company will grow, change, develop, and mold to let others clarify their purpose in life.

The original purpose to help people was correct. The second purpose is a more refined, pull-it-all-together resolution: have a happy and healthy company so I can bless people.

Chapter Two: Mission, Vision, Purpose

To go on a mission every day is awesome. You can choose if it's a scary mission, secret mission, thrilling mission, adventure mission, or... (Fill in the blank) mission. Create your own adventure. Every simple day starts with a journey. The secret is that EVERYONE is legendary. You earn the right to live by surrendering to a higher mission. Life is big. I live in creative imaginations. I am a Viking princess, I am the pin-up girl, I am the entrepreneur, I am an employment specialist, I am Green lantern!

I knew one of my missions in life was to be an employment specialist. Understanding the theory of how people pick their dream careers is so magical. During the current 13,557 days in my life so far, I have been on so many adventures/missions. Let's name a few: The mission of growth, the mission of happy, the mission of commitment, the mission of thriving, the mission of grievousness, the mission of a tribe, the mission of faith, the mission of healing, the mission of the win. The mission of wisdom, the mission of creating a satisfying life. The mission of true love, the mission of good, the mission of awakening, the mission of a hero, the mission of personal development, the mission of a phoenix, the mission of leaving a mark on this world. The mission of surrender, the mission of remaining happy, excited, and calm. The mission of blessing, the mission of mindset, the mission of treasure. The mission of beauty, grace, and glory. The mission of being bitter or better.

So many missions—our life mission does not have to be stagnant. It can change, learn, and grow. Can we go back to finish the first crush story? How does your first crush intertwine with creating a mission for your life?

Once you have a crush, your life naturally becomes obsessed with a mission to find out if they like you or not. You think about them day and night till you finally get to the reveal of understanding whether they like you or not. My first crush never loved me. I spent a good chunk of my time pursuing/thinking about him.

The mission of your life is the same way. It can be subconscious or unconscious. The conclusion to the story is that once I confronted my crush about him finding his true love, it was within six months that he was married to another amazing woman and got the title of Dad. Your mission affects other people's lives. What you do matters. Your mission matters.

Missions can change, grow, and develop. My mission at this point is to teach Career Development Classes. I love facilitating and teaching people to understand how to get their dream job. Since I run a company, this won't always be my mission. Missions are very much a choose your own adventure. The only question is, are you creating your mission or letting others create your mission?

Chapter Three: Find Your Treasure

The story of the treasure. I am on a hunt; I will find you. My treasure is success; my treasure is building a mindset that is phenomenally successful. I want the gold and the accolades. This whole week, the theme has been, "What is treasure?" I went on a treasure hunt on Friday where someone tried to steal me. Someone tried to control me and kidnap me. This is a real story. We did drugs...looked for a stupid treasure...he tried to make out with me and then drove me around Anthony Henday and would not drive me back to my car.

The sheer miracle – that he stopped, and I finally got out of the car – is unheard of in most dramatic suspense thrillers. This week I was living in trauma, and it had nothing to do with the pandemic. I am the treasure. You are a treasure as a human being. Love Yourself.

The mission was to look for treasure. The theme of this week was treasure. The treasure that I am hunting for is proper marketing in my company. The journey happened when I networked with over sixteen people this week. Three of them just forgot about me or had no time for me. Talk about a limiting belief—it's hard when people don't care about you.

The lion stalks its prey. It waits for you; it watches you. The evil in this world is watching you, tracking your every move. Are you getting eaten or fighting back?

What if you stalk back? Change the game... Be in the game. Win the mother### end game! Don't be naïve or claim self-fulfillment. Deception can eat it! Your light is uncomfortable for those hiding. Choose Joy, choose Peace, choose the epic adventure.

Chapter Three: Find Your Treasure

Words of Wisdom go a long way.

=Data Mine=

=Define your terms=

=Check your terms=

=Clarify your terms=

=Speak their language=

The pressure. There has been so much physical pressure/stress in my life this week. I don't like when I can't figure something out. I live in grace and peace. The feeling of pressure is uncomfortable. Growth is uncomfortable. How do you bend metal? You heat it up! Why do you heat it up? To refine it. In simple terms, the process of removing impurities. Similar to the word purification. In marketing, the right words are flawless and easy but in order to sell properly, theory has to be put in place. Wisdom. Ask for it, seek it out. I asked for wisdom, this is what I received...

=The treasure is GRACE and GLORY=

Define terms:

Glory – "Magnificent beauty"

Grace – "Simple elegance, refinement of movement, and cleverness"

Since we found the treasure early, it's important to look back at the confusion. The right answer or the wise answer. In my life, I have been given the power of epiphanies—clarifying the right answer but also stripping it down to the wise sage that resides within me. Let me share some of my treasures of life with you:

Chapter Three: Find Your Treasure

Happy Mothers Day, even if you are a male. Creation starts with a thought. You can be pregnant or and birth an idea. Men have babies in different ways. Businesses are babies at the beginning.

-I am always fighting...but I don't want to fight anymore. A good surrender goes a long way. Surrender to the magic of the universe.

-Breathe: breathe in, breathe out, repeat. You are blessed with life. Create a genesis of new life today.

-I am so uncomfortable. Growth is uncomfortable. If you hang out with me, I guarantee discomfort. We will fly, we will create a mind-blowing experience. New feelings will emerge, and you will be in a new world with new hope and renewed strength.

-The bottom line is SELF-CARE. Love yourself. Talk to yourself. Be your best friend.

-Where do we go from here?

-Where do we go for wisdom?

=The source=

Wisdom in the Bible is personified as a woman...

-Cleaning and refreshing concepts. How do we feed the soul? What cleanses and refreshes your life?

-Your life is 95% subconscious! Life is going on at a cellular level. You only get to create with 5% of your life. What are you creating?

Proverbs 1:2 – "Their purpose is to teach people wisdom and discipline, to help them understand the insights of the wise."

Proverbs 1: 32-33 – "For the waywardness of the simple will kill them, and the complacency of fools will destroy them; but whoever listens to me will live in safety and be at ease, without fear or harm."

Chapter Three: Find Your Treasure

Proverbs 2 – "My son, if you accept my words and store up my commands within you,
2 turning your ear to wisdom
and applying your heart to understanding—
3 indeed, if you call out for insight and cry aloud for understanding,
4 and if you look for it as for silver
and search for it as for hidden treasure,
5 then you will understand the fear of the Lord and find the knowledge of God.
6 For the Lord gives wisdom;
from his mouth come knowledge and understanding.
7 He holds success in store for the upright,
he is a shield to those whose walk is blameless,
8 for he guards the course of the just
and protects the way of his faithful ones.
9 Then you will understand what is right and just and fair—every good path.
10 For wisdom will enter your heart,
and knowledge will be pleasant to your soul.
11 Discretion will protect you,
and understanding will guard you.
12 Wisdom will save you from the ways of wicked men, from men whose words are perverse,
13 who have left the straight paths to walk in dark ways,
14 who delight in doing wrong
and rejoice in the perverseness of evil,
15 whose paths are crooked
and who are devious in their ways.
16 Wisdom will save you also from the adulterous woman, from the wayward woman with her seductive words,
17 who has left the partner of her youth
and ignored the covenant she made before God.
18 Surely her house leads down to death and her paths to the spirits of the dead.
19 None who go to her return or attain the paths of life.

Chapter Three: Find Your Treasure

20 Thus you will walk in the ways of the good and keep to the paths of the righteous.
21 For the upright will live in the land, and the blameless will remain in it;
22 but the wicked will be cut off from the land,
and the unfaithful will be torn from it."
HARK TO YOU; RECEIVE WISDOM. Receive your treasure. 2020 is over and we thrived. We built a mindset that was phenomenally successful. The full circle is GRACE and GLORY.

Grace: "Simple Elegance Glory, Magnificent Beauty"

Thank you!

Chapter Four: How Do You Market?

No one tells you marketing is a slow game. I am telling you... It's a slow game and you are never done marketing yourself.

Do you know what Career Development is? My name is Laurette Lee, the director/manager of Phoenix Career Development. I teach a program that is based on proper theories to get your dream job, and I have helped clients, students, immigrants, and people with disabilities understand how to plan their careers properly. I have worked with three non-profit companies that help clients change their lives. I am interested in a win-win theory. Can I email you some resources?

That is a strong elevator pitch and I use it all the time. The elevator pitch changes depending on what I want and what the client, customer, or business owner needs. You can be doing 95% of things right in your company and still not have clients. Marketing and running a company are a long play. There are plenty of failures.

=THE EPIPHANY=

I hate marketing. I hate telling people how amazing I am. I hate believing in my product and trying to convince others that they should buy my product. I do not want to be a shyster.

Marketing is not about you! It's never about me. It is about the consumer/client's pain problem. The client has questions about your product:

-What's in it for me?

-What will it cost?

Chapter Four: How Do You Market?

-What will I gain from this as a consequence?

-When will this happen?

-What guarantee are you offering?

Q: What is the pain problem in Phoenix Career Development?

A: People are unhappy with the career they have created for themselves.

They're really, really, really unhappy. There is no purpose in their career, and it does not satisfy them. It's about this time we talk about a belief in self. Do you believe you can get clients? Do you believe people will pay for your service?

The first "Yes" in my company came from the questions I brought forth to my mentor:

Me: "How do you do it? How do you actually do it? How do you get clients?"

Mentor response: "You just do it!"

Me: "I don't get 'You just do it!' What do you mean?"

The Backstory: The mentor gave me his script for selling. I knew what the script was since I had been practicing it.

The script:

=Understand your story/Understand your belief system=

=Understand the product=

=Ask questions=

=Understand your client=

=Get the clients to say "Yes," i.e., "Yes, you can solve their pain point." They say "Yes" to your question and your service.

=The call to action: Do you want the product? YES.

Chapter Four: How Do You Market?

Get people to say "Yes" to your product. "Yes" to the exchange of goods and services. Mentor: "Just do it: Get the client!"

Me: "Wait, wait, wait: All I have to do is believe I can get clients, and then I can get clients?"

Mentor: "YES!"

Me: "Fair, let's do this!"

This conversation happened at the end of March when everything just shut down because of the pandemic.

[The Claim] I am getting two clients this week because I believe in myself and my company.

[The result] A home run. I thrived just after the call for a shutdown. Two streams of income set up; I have a contract to write rehabilitation case notes for an insurance company and received my first client for Phoenix Career Development.

The deeper and deeper I get into marketing, the more it focuses on personal belief and clarifying your terms. So many people are speaking the same language yet the same words but different concepts within the words. Clarification is key to marketing. I start my elevator pitch with a question that you have to answer because I am clarifying terms, trying to get on the same page as you and matching your belief system. It's not manipulation—it's strategy.

The rabbit hole of concepts and definitions: client acquisition strategy, synergy, networking, partnerships, vision, mission, purpose, closing the deal, call to action, define your terms, authentic, the ask, build relationships, I heard a rumor, speak their language, marketing, campaign, etc.... It does not end; new concepts keep coming every day.

Let's talk about a Marketing Campaign:
Awareness: Hi, Hi, Hi, Hello
Get people's attention

Chapter Four: How Do You Market?

Interest: I help people find fulfillment in their careers. Do you or anyone you know have this pain point?

Engagement: Ask a question
Get the client talking.

Action: Specifically, a call to action
Will you use my service?

There is a simple flow to marketing. Done right, it is flawless and easy. It's like creating artwork, like a beautiful painting.

One of my Career Development classes is marketing yourself. You are a product! A darn good product. Only one of you exists. No one else can do what you do, the way you do it. I teach confidence in your skills, abilities, attributes, transferable skills, and values. Market yourself based on your values. Use business cards and the elevator pitch.

The key to marketing, again, is the other person. People do not buy your product; they buy the value/belief behind the product. Understand your belief so you can sell your product flawlessly. Confidence is magic.

<u>Client Acquisition Strategy</u>: A strategy to market. If you don't make a plan to market, you're not marketing.

Same But Different:

1. Interrupt
2. Engagement
3. Educate
4. Offer

1. Awareness
2. Interest
3. Engagement
4. Action

The first big phrase I learned in marketing was client acquisition strategy. What does that mean?

Answer: have a system in place to bring in new clients.

Chapter Four: How Do You Market?

My system so far:

A thirty-seconds elevator pitch

Flyers, videos, business cards. What is Career Development?

PowerPoint. The offer: Free What is Career Development?

And Career Planning...

Don't talk about money till you build trust with the client. Relationship building and sharing a belief has to happen before money. Ask lots of questions—it is not about you. It's always about the client. Yes, yes, yes, yes! The client needs to be on the same page as you. Finally, would you be interested in my service?

<u>Open Ended:</u>

Yes: YEAH!!!!

Or...

No: Not today
No: Too much
No: Just No

A "No" does not mean the relationship is over. Hesitations may still need to be addressed. Words of Wisdom:

Align with someone smarter than you.

My business coach is my business coach for a reason. In order to attract clients, you only need to do five things:

1. Advertise
2. Market
3. Direct Sales
4. Lead Generations: Target your Audience
5. Reviews and Testimonials

Chapter Four: How Do You Market?

To break down running a company even more, in business you should only be doing five things:

1. Monitor and Measure Cash Flow
2. Time thinking about your business
3. Sell every day
4. Market
5. Have a Plan

Feelings come into play. You have to market with feelings. Some people market with deception, others with cunning and charm. How do you want to market yourself? Being an entrepreneur, you live and breathe work. You are thinking about marketing all the time. =ALL THE TIME=

Help along the way – Along with a business coach, have a tribe of business owners that have been in the game longer than you and are far more successful. Ninja Marketing was created for that reason. Every Friday between the hours of 2-4 pm, I take classes on marketing my business. Learn and grow. In life, you are never done being amazing and marketing yourself. Life is standing up for your beliefs and sharing them with others.

Let's talk about energy. Everything is made up of energy. Marketing is energy, money is energy, you as a person are energy. The law of attraction is a secondary law in life. Understand that in marketing there are forces at work that you cannot see. The primary law is the law of vibration. Market yourself in a whisper campaign and an "I heard a rumor" campaign. My individual branding in life is legendary. My tribe always drops my name with the legendary Laurette Lee— she runs Phoenix Career Development. Step into your role and be bold.

My favorite marketing tag lines:

Business: Find where your potential thrives.
    Personal: Slay some dragons and go on a journey of epic proportions. Life is not about the finish line. Life is about enjoying the journey.

Chapter Four: How Do You Market?

This Chapter will finish with an encouragement sponsored by my Dad:

"There will always be somebody better at the one thing you're good at, but no one in the universe can reach the quality of your combination of talents, ideas, abilities, and feelings."

"Through all of eternity, no one will ever look, talk, walk, think, or do like you. You're special...you're rare. And in all your rarity there is great value. Because of your great value, you need not attempt to imitate others."

"You will accept and, yes, celebrate your differences. You're special and you are beginning to realize it's no accident that you are special."

"You're beginning to see that God made you special for a purpose. He must have a job for you that no one else can do as well as you. You are special."

—Letter from Dad

Final Thoughts: You're amazing; you deserve to market yourself flawlessly. Tell the world.

Chapter Five: The Unicorn Finds Her Tribe

I am from the generation of being special. We did get trophies just for showing up. Man, that did not prepare me for "real life." Growing up, I longed so hard for people to like and understand me. All I got was, "You're weird." The unicorn in me knew I was not like other people. I stood out, talked differently, thought differently, acted differently, lived my life differently, and was highly unique. Even though I am a twin sister, we both are very similar but very different. I heard a rumor that people have tribes. People share similar beliefs with others and form groups.

When I was a child, the basic theology my mother bestowed on me is that there are Christians and then there are "Christians." I didn't fit in with the Christians. It was a weird feeling to believe in your core—Christ died for your sins and all you had to do was accept Christ as your savior, and then you are saved. Christianity was almost a solo journey for me. I am a Christian because God is alive, real, and active in my life. I don't need to debate it, and, in my life, God is in control. I am surrendered to a higher purpose.

Why is it so hard to "fit into" the mold of society? The best Mom line is, "Normal is just a setting on a hair dryer." I just thought everyone in life was faking this belonging to a group. In my head, the unicorn itself was alone, single, solo. She really did want to belong; she just never did.

I have a hard time trusting people. I have a hard time finding mentors. I have a hard time thinking other people are better than I am. My Canadian cultural belief is equality. People are neither better nor less than others. That thought made me have a hard time putting people on a pedestal. Part of a tribe is that different members come to the table with different skill sets.

Chapter Five: The Unicorn Finds Her Tribe

The first tribe I was ever a part of was family. You're stuck with those guys. I did not choose them. I still love them, but they are not my choice of tribe. I wanted to choose where I belonged in society. In life, your second tribe is usually your work family. The unicorn in me made me easy to spot. People spotted me as something like, "She's cool, but... (dot, dot, dot)" I found work was a testing ground; a trial for developing my skills, qualities, attributes, and core values. I never deeply bonded with work family. I found a lot of people were just working for a paycheck and to get their basic needs met. Work tribes didn't care about the individual.

The next tribe was the "friend tribe." Again, being a twin, Lindsey was my default friend. I loved her but she was my sister. Lindsey might have hindered me from forming a friend tribe. I was not a very social person. Communicating with others was hard and awkward. You cannot have a tribe with two members. This is just the definition of twins. I always make one friend, never a tribe. I don't know how people do it. It took me 36 years to find my girlfriend tribe, and it's the best story ever. I love the dream team. The dream team is bigger than me. The dream team is a concept where my girlfriends and I encourage, support, love, and push ourselves to discomfort.

A theme that keeps coming up in my life is that in order to care for others you must first look after yourself. Personal development is key to finding a tribe.

Tribe, tribe, tribe, tribe, tribe: Define the term as "a social division in a traditional society consisting of families or communities linked by social, economic, religious, or blood ties, with a common culture and dialect and typically having a recognized leader."

I created a house of ruin. Slowly, the disintegration of my life came to be complete. The funny thing is that within desecration is liberation. I started to love myself. I started to stand up for myself. I choose me; my core values and beliefs were so strong, it was me vs. them. People live in self-sacrifice or self-sabotage all the time. I was switching the narrative of life to thriving, winning the race. When we change perspectives, we change not only the rules of the game, but we also change the game altogether.

Chapter Five: The Unicorn Finds Her Tribe

When Phoenix Career Development was in the gestation stage, I was learning what it meant to be an entrepreneur. I put a lot of weight on my husband/boyfriend (we were never actually married) to do the marketing and selling of Phoenix Career Development. I thought he was going to be my ride or die. I loved him so deeply, he was a soul mate. The deeper we got into launching my company, the more pushback I got from him. He was always short with me. I became his enemy. If you ask him why we broke up he will tell you I joined a cult and was abusive toward him. Perspective is everything. I refuse to make him the enemy. I leveled up; nothing could stop me from being successful, including someone that self-sabotages without their knowledge. I broke up with him in mid-March of 2020. Then the pandemic hit. The next week I obtained my first two contracts in my company. I thrived in a pandemic.

The chapter is about finding your tribe but, again, in order to find your tribe, you also have to remove toxic people from your life.

Jan 3-5, 2020 – I went to personal development classes. They talked about finding your tribe and dealing with your demons. The Ex thought the classes were cultish. Define terms: "A cult is a system of religious veneration and devotion directed toward a particular figure or object. A small group of people having religious beliefs or practices regarded by others as strange or sinister." Personal development is not a cult—a sect maybe, but not a cult.

The attribute within me changed. The huge epiphany was I didn't love myself. I was mean to myself. The solution: Ten "I AM" statements about how amazing I am and ten gratitudes every day. Also, share with others every day; share the journey of awesome. Megan Pacholuk and Marah-May were part of this group of ladies. I would Marco Polo them every night just before I went to bed. The girls are a blessing, and we give each other permission to dream new dreams—the tribe of the dream team came into play. These ladies understand they are growing old with me. We will always encourage, love, and support each other.

Once it rains, it pours. Starting a business, I knew I needed checks and balances. I needed people that were smarter and have been in the game of

Chapter Five: The Unicorn Finds Her Tribe

business longer than I have. Anderson Career Training Institute had a 16-week mentorship at the end of their program. Joe and Sandy were my mentors. They were amazing. I learned a lot over the first 16 weeks of launching my business. I learned about the long play, believe in self, and battling your inner demons. Most businesses fail the first year, and it makes sense why—you are your biggest saboteur. When my 15 weeks were ending, I needed to find a tribe ASAP. Last year I was dipping my feet into BNI's, (Business Network International) EBA's (Edmonton business Association), and cyndicate.org.

BNI's were way too structured. YUCK. Business should be fun. Also, I use my morning for quiet intentions, goal setting, and visualizing the future; not for networking. My A-game is not at 6: 30 in the morning. EBA was super-old people. I respect them but I didn't want to be a part of something where everyone knew the answers but me. I wanted to find a business group that was, well, a tribe.

I was on the hunt. I was searching. I went to a how-to market on YouTube, an event sponsored by Rapid Boost Marketing. Ali was amazing, and he knew his stuff. Post every day, post often, post like it's a workout routine. Because I went to that event in real life, my FB popped up a cyndicate meeting on zoom. No one introduced me to cyndicate; I was looking for it. It was destiny, and for those people that believe in the law of attraction, this is the best example of it.

At the first cyndicate meeting, a spark in my soul happened. Mitch Cammidge is the business coach that runs Tribe One meetings. Within minutes of starting the networking meeting, he dropped the word "tribe."

Mitch: "Welcome to Tribe One. We are a family of business owners that grow businesses and build personal relationships within."

My goal in this meeting was to talk to everyone, especially the quiet ones—they have the most secrets.

From that one meeting, I got 17 zoom meetings a week for three months straight. It was really neat how some people asked me to have a meeting.

Chapter Five: The Unicorn Finds Her Tribe

Attraction happens eventually but not to start with. It makes sense that most companies fail in their first year.

I knew Mitch was a tribe leader, and I didn't feel comfortable talking to him before I talked to others in the group. I think I talked to 20 people before he actually headhunted me to have a conversation. It was my time to shine, my time to impress a titan in the field. The meeting was set for 9:00 am on a Wednesday morning. I woke up at 7:00 am, had a run, dressed up like a pinup girl, and did my goal-setting, intention settings, and blessings for the day.

> Mitch: "How did you get here?"
> Me: "Umm, to be honest, I don't know how to answer that question."
> Mitch: "Let's scale back. How are you doing?"
> Me: "I am the stuff of legend. They will write stories about me! I came to play, I came to impress, I came to run an empire."
> Mitch: "How are you going to do that?"
> Me: "Honestly, I don't know… that is why I joined cyndicate.org."

Mitch and I believe in Win-Win. We believe in caring for our tribe and being "SAVAGE IN BUSINESS." That was really fun to find a business coach that is a warrior poet. We both use creative imagination and storytelling. The unicorn has changed into a Viking Princess and found her tribe, and she gets to slay dragons every day. The dragons of business, marketing, and running an empire can be slaughtered with a tribe.

Within a tribe, you can also have sub-tribes. Ninja marketing is also a group of people I meet with once a week to learn how to market and build a plan for making my company successful. My company, Phoenix Career Development, needs a dream team, needs a syndicate, and needs a ninja marketing expert. Find your tribe…Love your tribe.

=Be Blessed=

Chapter Six: The Healing Journey

No one tells you that a journey is quiet. No one tells you that most of the time the routines of healing are boring. I want to tell you about the healing of boredom. Define boring as "not interesting—tedious." Let us switch the term; let's create a reaction to boring. My definition of boring is "a call to action." Being boring means your creative imagination needs to come into play. Those moments of waking up every morning knowing I had a serious heart condition were a blessing. It was not scary to know at any second, I could die. It was peace!

The Tattoo: When I turned 28, I got my Surrender tattoo. I knew when I was 18 I wanted this ink on my body. When I was 34, I almost died; I surrendered. The prophecy of my life was, "No, No, No. You don't get the pleasure of death at this moment—you get the pure pleasure of life at this moment. Death is easy, life is hard, but it's also the fun part." I smiled after the gentle peace of a wake-up from all the beeping around me. My man was so worried about me. He ran to me and did not sleep the next two days. He just stayed with me. This was a moment in my life where I knew a New Chapter was about to be exposed.

People are here in our life for a season. I learned my "ride or dies" in my life are my twin sister, Megan Booger, and the boyfriend. He earned his stripes to stay with me for a season. Seven days in the hospital—name the problem: CARDIOMYOPATHY. The doctor gave me three choices about how my life could go:

1. DIE: UMMM, NO.
2. Stay the same: UMM, Still No.
3. Get Better = I choose # three.

Chapter Six: The Healing Journey

Start the solution/Start the healing journey:

=Set Intention: I will heal from this completely =

When I got home the heart doctor set me on an exercise routine:

-Day One: Please do a 10-minute exercise of walking
-Day Two: Please do a 20-minute exercise of walking
-Day Three: Please do a 30-minute exercise of walking (you can break it up as long as the total is 30   minutes)
-Day Four: Please do a 40-minute exercise of walking (you can break it up as long as the total is 40 minutes)-Day Five: Please do a 50-minute exercise of walking (you can break it up as long as the total is 50 minutes)
-Day Six: Please do a 60-minutes of exercise of walking (you can break it up as long as the total is 60 minutes)

REACH THE ROUTINE: Reach the boring of routine. This is my point; routine is not boring. Routine is a blessing.

Talk about breathing. Before entering the hospital, I struggled so hard for breath. I cannot explain what it is like to understand the normalcy of struggling for breath. The first year of healing, at least three times a day I struggled to breathe. The second year of healing, at least once a day I struggled to breathe. This moment, being year two and nine months of healing, when I am worried, scared, and nervous, it is hard to breathe. Let's talk about feelings. Healthy feelings: happiness, joy, excitement. Feelings are a Superpower; feelings are a call to action. When we are sad it is a call to action for understanding.

We are whole-body creatures: Mind, Body, and Soul. When we cut one of these out, we cut ourselves off from our unlimited potential. The first year of healing was peace; not just peace but gentle peace. I was on short-term disability for four months. So, money was taken care of, and I only had to worry about my healing. Find miracles along the way. In my job, I always wanted to run to another company for stability but a little voice inside

Chapter Six: The Healing Journey

myself said, This is where you stay. That is the first time my intuition told me to stay at a job.

Thank goodness I did...disability money is a blessing.

The day I almost died in the hospital is the day I asked for a puppy. I saved 250 bucks every paycheck of my disability for four months. Azazel was born the day I asked for a puppy in the hospital.

The Healing Journey tip #1: Routine

The Healing Journey tip #2: Thoughts and feelings

The Healing Journey tip #3: A network of people and what you surround yourself with

Healing is painful; a heartbeat is a gift. I started to have an interest in the sound of a healthy

heart—thud, thud, thud. A baby's heartbeats run faster than an adult's. The first time I put puppy Azazel's heart up against mine to feel her life force, it was painful. I was weak.

The Healing Journey tip #4: A heartbeat

After four months of being on disability and being ready to go back to OSP, I got unemployed again. I help people with disabilities get jobs, and once I got a disability, I got unemployed. That is the definition of interesting. I knew an epic job existed for me. I was not going back to death; I was going toward full abundance.

A five-dollar raise is a thing of legend. I got it and started working with immigrants to help them plan their careers in Canada. I loved every second of that job. I believe in supporting and encouraging. The boyfriend's time was about to shine. I was living my dreams and it was time for him to live in grace, glory, and blessing. We did the math; I would be making a little less than our income together for the last five years. He wanted to go back to school and become an emergency manager. I supported his dreams because he supported me with my healing journey.

Chapter Six: The Healing Journey

Another ending—my contract was for eight months. I knew the only way for me to have stability in life was to create my own. Miracle! A good connection goes a long way. J and K Career Services were looking for English Teachers. I applied for the English Teacher job because I just needed an "in" for an interview. That interview has nothing to do with being a teacher. My agenda for that meeting was to see how someone else became a manager of a company. I wanted to job shadow an Entrepreneur.

The Thought:

How is it possible for an immigrant with no experience as an employment specialist to give advice to others to get a job in Canada? If he can run a company, I can run a company.

The Healing Journey tip #5: Give Permission for Creative Imagination

The thought of running my own company sustained me for 6 months. It was the best thought I have ever created.

The Healing Journey tip #6: Thoughts

I can heal from a heart condition. I can run my own company.

The Healing Journey tip #7: The Power of Words

Start writing and thinking about the condition as disassociated from me. Instead of my heart condition, it becomes a heart condition. So many people live in love with their chronic pain. People use their pain as pity. Pity is weak. However, there is strength in weakness. Be broken. Be weak.

Change of thoughts: In my early 20s, I was swimming in the ocean; barely surviving. I was drowning.

Thirty-four years old and I was drowning in water in my lungs and life was survive or die; simple— no more, no less. In the hospital, I needed a new survival thought... head out in a rowboat? No, no, no—not big enough or safe... Hop on a cruise ship of the mind.

A thought goes a long way. A thought goes into action. A thought causes another one and another one...and another one. I was not making money

Chapter Six: The Healing Journey

at J & K Career Service. It was a month-long job shadow working for free (some money under the table) but not enough. I needed an emergency job. Concordia University as an admissions advisor. I asked the Universe for a Rocky moment, to get a job for four months and then have some money to invest in my own company. I heard a rumor that successful people think differently. I heard a rumor some people thrive. I heard a rumor you can build a mindset that is highly successful.

The Healing Journey tip #8: Learn new things

Read. Part of healing is to be open to learning. At Concordia, I listened to 37 books, including *As a Man Thinketh* by Viktor Franke, *Think and Grow Rich* by Napoleon Hill, *Rich Dad Poor Dad* by Robert Kiyosaki and Sharon Lechter, *The Game of Life and How to Play It* by Florence Scovel Shinn. Concordia graciously wanted to extend my contract, but I politely said, "No, thank you. I have a dream, a calling, a mission that I must claim." Once unemployed, I reached out to Anderson Career Training Institute to learn how to be an Entrepreneur. I have the mindset, and I just needed some nitty-gritty knowledge to be off and running.

The Healing Journey tip #9: Define your terms On the first day at Anderson, we learned about entrepreneurs: "A person that organizes and operates a business." My mind was shattered. A pattern of belief was fighting back. I did not believe in myself. I did not love myself.

The Healing Journey tip #10: Share a Secret

In class one day I noticed someone was simply different from other people—he had a secret. He was powerful, mystic, understood networks, and was a force to be reckoned with. I flat out asked him, "What is your secret?" Instead of telling me, he posed a challenge. "What are you doing January 3-5th, 2020?" Me: "Nothing! Ohh, a free class..." Personal development is key to healing. Talk to yourself. This class pivoted my life at this point.

Chapter Six: The Healing Journey

The Healing Journey tip # 11: Belief in Self

I went on a soul journey, opened a treasure, and got the best reward—a belief in self. The journey, the epiphany, the reason I got a heart condition is I did not love myself. I was mean to love myself.

The Healing Journey tip # 12: Love Yourself

-Take Care of Yourself-

Phoenix Career Development launched on January 28, 2020, and then a pandemic hit. I have worked hard on healing. I was already in success energy; my healing thought was more magical than a pandemic. I thrived in COVID.

The Journey is almost at an end. Let's recap Healing Tips:

1. Be boring: In a moment of boredom is peace and happiness
2. Feelings and thoughts are superpowers
3. A network of people and what you surround yourself with matters
4. A heartbeat
5. Give permission for creative imagination
6. Thought: I can heal my heart
7. The power of words. Dissociate from the problem
8. Learn new things
9. Define your terms
10. Share a secret: Personal Development
11. Belief in self
12. Love yourself

Closing thoughts: Today I live on an island. It is safe! It lets me network and meet new people. It lets me enjoy and live on a vacation consistently. One day soon I will get off this island and move to my own creative imagination house with my three rental properties. Complete healing is upon us. Do I claim it? Yes. July 13, 2020 at 11 am my heart doctor will say. "You slew the dragon of self-hate. You are healed." The heart condition has weakened my muscle. The heart is a muscle the size of your fist.

Keep on loving. Keep on fighting.

Hold on, Hold on, Hold on for your life.

Chapter Seven: Pattern Beliefs

The more I get into business the more I learn about myself. Since we know that life is 95% subconscious and 5% conscious, what are we telling ourselves? We have a vested interest in self-talk and self-motivation. At the end of the day, our self-program affects us deeply. We decide if we are thriving or surviving. Most companies fail in the first year for the sole reason of self. We are enemies of our successful mindset. When my company was launching, I knew the only way to be successful was to build a mindset that was highly successful. But how do we do it? Everything also goes back to problem-solving skills.

(Mr. Google): "How do you solve a problem?" Seven effective problem-solving skills:

1. Identify the issue. Be clear about what the problem is…
2. Understand everyone's interest
3. List the possible solutions (options)
4. Evaluate the options…
5. Select an option or options
6. Document the agreement
7. Agree on contingencies, monitoring, and evaluation

Continual pattern beliefs block me. Even today I was too hard on myself. I am mean to myself. I am not my biggest fan. This is where mantras, meditations, and affirmations come into play.

"Laurette, you got this; Laurette, be nice to yourself."

"Pattern Believes Money"

Chapter Seven: Pattern Beliefs

The biggest pattern belief I wrestle with is my company—I fear money. It's embarrassing being scared of money. Honestly, it hit me in my bathroom, I fell on the floor and just started crying. I had a flashback of my Dad yelling at me because I asked why he never had time for me.

His passion for supporting his family by working diligently shone through his snarled scream—spit flying out of his mouth and the deep red of anger on his face. I just wanted him to spend time with me. You can't spend time with those you love if you are too busy supporting them.

Loneliness and rejection are huge pattern beliefs I am still working on... On top of choosing to support us financially, it caused my dad to reject us on a daily basis, and because of this, I felt lonely.

No pity party at this moment. My dad is amazing; his sacrifice taught me that rejection does not mean people dismiss others because they are inadequate. People reject people for lots of reasons. A good rejection was a sacrifice for having a father that did support me. No matter what, even if he couldn't physically hang out with me, he always supported me in a different way.

The problem-solving skills of breaking down my pattern beliefs of being scared of money: 1– Identify the issue: The fact of the matter is I am scared to make money. 2 – Understand everyone's interest. It's time to face my fear; you can make money and not sacrifice quality time with family. 3 – Possible solutions: New Mantras—"Money flows to me easily" and "I use my wealth to bless people." 4 – Evaluate options: Mantras are working. I am slowly getting clients. 5 – Select options: Mantras are working along with a belief in self.

Add the mantra, "I am building a mindset that is highly successful." 6 – Document the agreement: This is pretty much why I am writing this book. Life changes very quickly or very slowly—enjoy the ride. You only get one day like the present. 7 – Monitor my progress: I have to be diligent to do my mantras. It's very easy for me to slip back into poor, broken, drowning me; I have conversations with myself constantly, practice slowing. Do

Chapter Seven: Pattern Beliefs

gratitudes, blessings, intention settings, and visualize the future in order for new pattern beliefs to emerge.

Let's name all the pattern beliefs that Laurette has shattered this year: no self-love, hard on self, speeding through life, fear money, not good enough, not successful, old me, organized chaos... They just keep coming.

It seems like if I address one pattern belief, a new one pops up in its place. Life is full of Phoenix Moments. We break in order to rise from the ashes to start another day. Every day is a new journey, a new game, a new life to be created.

Let's talk about the princess pattern beliefs. As little girls, everyone wanted to be rescued by a prince. I never wanted to be rescued... Honestly, I wanted to be the star of the show: The Laurette Show. She was entertaining and enlightened; there were sparklers and thought-provoking content. Before YouTube, I was a star in my own right, and all my friends would come and watch the next episode of "The Laurette Show." Thirteen episodes and two seasons later, it didn't get canceled. I fell in love.

Within me, I have a beast and a domesticated animal. I love being mature, proper, and having a deep understanding of theology. I also love burping, jeans and a t-shirt, being dirty, and letting my inner animal run wild. I am a wild card within routine and grace.

It is so easy to lose yourself. It's so easy to feel comfortable in life. The last pattern belief to talk about is Authentic Self. Almost every single entrepreneur's top value in their company is authenticity. What does it actually mean? Define Terms: "of undisputed origin, genuine."

My authentic self is determined by duality—the wolf of extravert and introvert, domesticated or wild. Both are essentially raw, real, and emotionally me. I need both to function as a happy healthy adult. When I feed one more than the other, I am unbalanced and self-destructive. It took me a long time to understand and even discover this about myself.

Chapter Seven: Pattern Beliefs

1. Identify the issue:

Be clear on what the problem is. The problem is self-acceptance and finding a balance in my life. The Pattern Belief is loving me just the way I am and accepting what I must share with the world.

I am wild; I am weird

I am professional; I am childish; I am a beast

I am an introvert; I am highly social; I am domesticated

2. Understand everyone's interest:

If I feed the Domestic Creature, I am a workaholic. If I feed the wild beast, I am immature. My interest is that I need both sides of me to thrive. If I starve one, I can't support myself, or else I'm unhappy and depressed in life. My interest is that I have lived both extremes and my best life resides somewhere in the middle, i.e., a balance of self.

Authenticity is difficult because you have to discover who you are in order to break the pattern belief. I have to be intentional about loving myself, listening to myself, and finding a balance in my bilateral nature.

3. Possible solutions:

Peace and distraction of self.

4. Evaluate Options:

Living as the beast all the time gets me in trouble. Living as domestic all the time makes me unhappy. The only option is to find a happy medium. Love each chapter of me and share experiences with both of my Gemini natures. The last option is peace and surrender. Relaxing and understanding life is a journey, not a destination. Arrive at the present and enjoy.

Chapter Seven: Pattern Beliefs

5. Select an Option:

For me, the only option is surrender. I am tired of running the race. The game of life is not a race. The game of life is how you create it. Create a satisfying life. What does it look like when the tenacious beast within gets to play and the domestic qualities in my life get to feel safe? Stability is the greatest with the peace of surrender.

6. Document the agreement:

Again, one of the reasons I am writing this book. You get one year of opening a company— might as well enjoy the experience by writing a book called "A Journey of Epic Proportions."

7. Agree on Contingencies, Monitoring, and Evaluations:

This is where surrender comes from. We sometimes can't see grace and glory because we are in the muck and mire: gratitude work, mindset work, belief in self-work, best-part-of-my-day work, goal-setting work, intentions work, and, lastly, blessings work. We are enough.

Pattern beliefs come and grow in our lives. We can break them, we can stay in them, and we can love them. Pattern beliefs are our faith in life. We use our faith when we are tested with extreme crises. We need to be dependent on a higher being to help us break bad pattern beliefs in life. Perseverance is key: Surrender, Surrender, Surrender, live a road less traveled one step at a time and become legendary. We have to have obedience to routine and obedience to trust and obey the universe, God, Christ, -FILL IN THE BLANK- because to be honest, there is no other way. Lastly, SURRENDER.

Chapter Eight: Bullet Journal

As we start the eighth chapter, it is important to assess what is important for you. What are your top values in life?

Write them below:

1.

2.

3.

4.

My top values are:

1. Sense of purpose
2. Humor and playfulness
3. Creativity, ingenuity, and being original
4. Leadership

This book was created to spark your interest in what your Career Development looks like. Are you happy in your chosen field? If the answer is "Yes!" that is awesome, and the tips/tricks I share in this chapter will be a refresher for you. I find simplicity and going back to the basics are important structures on which to build your dream career.

Chapter Eight: Bullet Journal

When I was on the growing edge last year, I started to write in journals. It was messy, unorganized, and without structure. Sometimes the best thing to do is just start and do it wrong the first time. I would not even say my first journal was messy (Bahahaha, it was so bad...), it just needed some organization.

This is how I create my journals....

You need: The best part of your day, ten Gratitudes, Blessings, Goal Settings, Intention Settings, Visual Futures, "I AM" STATEMENTS, going deep with five questions, and a month to learn and dwell on a concept.

<u>Gratitudes</u> are a superpower. Ten gratitudes a day change your perspective on life. Instead of letting life suck right in front of your face, it gives you the power to switch the narrative in your life, to start being thankful for the life you were given.

Day 1   Day 2

1.   1.
2.   2.
3.   3.
4.   4.
5.   5.
6.   6.
7.   7.
8.   8.
9.   9.
10.   10.

Chapter Eight: Bullet Journal

Day 3

1.
2.
3.
4.
5.
6.
7.
8.
9.
10.

Day 4

1.
2.
3.
4.
5.
6.
7.
8.
9.
10.

Turnaround is fair play. I would never let the reader do something I would never do...These are some of my Gratitude days:

1. Taxes
2. Websites
3. Marketing
4. NLP
5. Meditations
6. Healing Energy
7. Friends

1. Smiles
2. Tears
3. Cuddles
4. Books
5. Creative Imagination
6. Poems
7. Exercise

Chapter Eight: Bullet Journal

8.	Vacations	8. Puppy Licks
9.	Clients	9. Risk and Reward
10.	Hugs	10. Story Tellers

1. Green Lantern	1. Breathing
2. A Journey of Epic Proportions	2. The Wild Beast Within
3. Phoenix Career Development	3. Money
4. Integrity	4. Faith
5. Hope	5. Love
6. Grace	6. Glory
7. SURRENDER	7. Lay Down Burdens
8. Sparklers	8. Cookies
9. Stability	9. Azazel
10. Argos	10. ME

Gratitudes are difficult when you start, but they do get easier and easier. If it's a difficult day to do gratitudes, then those are the days you really need them.

I mash together the goal setting, blessings, intention settings, visualizing the future, and the best part of my day.

<u>Blessings</u>: Define Terms: "God's Favor and Protection"

O.K., O.K., O.K.—this is a hot button if you're not a believer! Blessings can just mean A Little Gift from Heaven. Do you look for gifts in your world? Do you look for abundance in the everyday? I love a good blessing. I love looking for them, I love finding them, I love receiving them.

Blessings: Releasing and letting go of my old ways

Blessings: Health and happiness

Blessings: Boys!

Blessings: Men

Blessings: PUPPIES

Blessings: Sister, family

Blessings: More than enough

Blessings: Friendships

Blessings: Breathing

Blessings: Naps

Goal Setting: Define Terms: "involves the development of an action plan designed to motivate and guide a person or group toward the desired result." Set one goal this day! Make it a good one and accomplish it. It can be as easy as putting on socks. I am not looking for a miracle; that already happened by you being you.

Enjoy your accomplishments.

Goal Setting: NLP

Goal Setting: Finish a chapter

Goal Setting: Website

Goal Setting: Drink some tea today

Goal Setting: How to Cold Call video

Chapter Eight: Bullet Journal

Goal Setting: Enjoy the day

Goal Setting: Slay meetings

Goal Setting: Finish RFP

Goal Setting: Surrender to the day

Goal Setting: Sit and DO

<u>Intention Settings</u>: Define Terms: "Intention is a thing to aim or plan for." We set intentions because as humans we should be asking ourselves why we are here on Earth. What is my mindset this morning?

100 days of Intention Settings: A little look into three months of my Legendary Journey

1. Know your outcomes
2. Choose your adventure
3. Today is a good day to slay
4. Every sunshine starts with a journey
5. Slay some dragons
6. I am happy, healthy, and blessed
7. I am hungry for Knowledge, Wisdom, (Fill in the blank)
8. Better or bitter
9. Create a satisfying life
10. I am successful
11. I win the race
12. Visualize the future
13. Play in creative imagination

14. Gold Standard: Goal Settings, Intention Settings, and Blessings

15. Mantra Time

16. Wisdom: Ask Lady Wisdom

17. What is your deepest passion? Play with it!

18. What is your favorite childhood memory?

19. Play in creative imagination (your ideal life)

20. Your epic life looks like…

21. Life is meaningful

22. You have a divine mind

23. Destroy fear, =CONFIDENCE=

24. Put first things first

25. You have to believe it can be done

26. Win-Win

27. Be transformed by the renewing of your mind

28. Power and abundance

29. Believe, Believe, Believe—faith to move mountains!

30. The heart is a symbol of creative activities

31. The dreamers are the heroes of the world

32. Hold your goals with tenacity

33. Recession vs. abundance

34. Be the pioneer you are

35. I am living the life I deserve

36. Life is easy, lucrative, and fun

Chapter Eight: Bullet Journal

37. Life is exciting, peaceful, and abundant
38. You master your craft
39. Be the titan in your field
40. Your pilgrimage is calling
41. Be a unicorn
42. Design your dream life
43. Be the hero in your own life
44. Find where your potential thrives
45. I heard a rumor: "You can do it"
46. Destroy fear, build your life
47. Create the magic within
48. Learning to get to a place where your unconscious becomes competent
49. I am not invisible. I exist.
50. The Universe is designed to trigger you
51. Peacefulness and bliss are the core of humanity
52. The best gifts are attitude and gratitude
53. The power of choice, the power of words
54. Shape a genesis week from the chaos of life
55. Vulnerability is the birthplace of innovation
56. You are the solution to the problem
57. Belief in self goes a long way
58. Deal with your self-patterned beliefs

59. Think differently; think often
60. The power of a name
61. Learn to be open; make some mistakes
62. I believe in right here, right now! Breathe.
63. Set the stage: visualize the future, play the game, set the game
64. Authentic self
65. Self-development: mantras, attitudes, and gratitudes
66. Healing energy vs. sick energy: everything is matter
67. Be open to the adventure of life
68. Your word is your wand
69. Your voice and your opinions are gifts to this world
70. Get yourself in front, before they need you!
71. Success is a mindset
72. Hold your goals with tenacity
73. Be impeccable with your words
74. Heart desires
75. Exercise your right to succeed!
76. Build a belief in self
77. Seek first to understand who you are
78. Make daily victories
79. Create a success picture
80. You are a hero
81. Unlimited potential

Chapter Eight: Bullet Journal

82. Build a highly successful mindset
83. Take action
84. Put on armor
85. Magic is in the air
86. The hard conversations
87. Create a story from a blank paper
88. I got sunshine
89. Ask for wisdom
90. Rainbow dancing unicorns
91. The meaning of life: To pursue human flourishing through communication, understanding, and service
92. Calmness is power
93. Give permission to ask questions
94. Make failure your best friend
95. Practice slowing
96. Love yourself
97. Level-up
98. Be on death ground on purpose
99. Focus on the healing Journey

Next: Stop in silence

Visualize the future: For reality to become real, you have to believe in it; you have to see it. How do you see the future? You write it down. You look at it. You Visualize it!!!! Live in creative imagination—sometimes your brain cannot comprehend if you are living in the past, present, or future. You are the only one who creates your future.... Do a good job!

Visualize Future: 10 clients a day; 10,000 dollars
Visualize Future: 2 clients this week
Visualize Future: B.C. home, amazing friends
Visualize Future: I got the RFP
Visualize Future: 10 clients; 10,000 dollars
Visualize Future: A good night's sleep
Visualize Future: Best holiday ever
Visualize Future: Mind-blowing, cool home
Visualize Future: Build a fierce network
Visualize Future: Enjoy the ride of life

AND THE BEST PART OF MY DAY: At the end of the day, it is important to capture this moment and this time. Nothing is more sacred than being alive and in this moment. The best part of my day makes me choose the best moment so that not all of my day was hectic, chaotic, and crazy. Are you recapping your day and looking at it with love and adventure?

The best part of my day:

- Quiet
- Seeing my son Pax
- Sleep
- Dog cuddles
- New mattress

Chapter Eight: Bullet Journal

- Bro talk
- Sex
- Bath time: new beginnings
- The show-up
- Cookies

This is "Fill in the blank" time– Mornings:

Day 1

Goal Setting:

Intentions Settings:

Blessings:

Day 2

Goal Setting:

Intention Settings:

Blessings:

Day 3

Goal Setting:

Intentions Settings:

Blessings:

Day 4

Goal Setting:

Intention Settings:

Blessings:

Day 5

Goal Setting:

Intentions Settings:

Blessings:

Day 6

Goal Setting:

Intention Settings:

Blessings:

Day 7

Goal Setting:

Intentions Settings:

Blessings:

Chapter Eight: Bullet Journal

Day 8

Goal Setting:

Intention Settings:

Blessings:

This is "Fill in the blank" time – Nighttime:

Day 1

Visualize Future:

Best part of your day:

Day 2

Visualize Future:

Best part of your day:

Day 3

Visualize Future:

Best part of your day:

Chapter Eight: Bullet Journal

Day 4

Visualize Future:

Best part of your day:

Day 5

Visualize Future:

Best part of your day:

Day 6

Visualize Future:

Best part of your day:

Day 7

Visualize Future:

Best part of your day:

Day 8

Visualize Future:

Best part of your day:

It's officially your adventure. How do you want to choose your own adventure? I switch it up every once in a while and will focus on other things to learn about during my holy hour of meditations.

Chapter Eight: Bullet Journal

The "I AM" statements force you to be nice to yourself and start encouraging your core self. I started the year with 3 weeks of affirmations. Looking at all my affirmations I set out for 2020, they were all slaughtered and gave me huge confidence to deal with a whirlwind, unprecedented exploit of my first year in business.

Ten "I AM" statements:

Laurette is grateful for calmness

Laurette is confident

Laurette has security in Christ

Laurette has security in money

Laurette has solutions to other people's problems

Laurette is strong

Laurette is abundance

Laurette is grateful

Laurette is free

Laurette is loving

WHAT ARE YOUR I AM STATEMENTS?...

Gratitudes are like Level One in self-mastery. Level Two in self-mastery is "I AM" statements. You will never be ready for "I am" Statements if you are still looking to understand yourself. If you are, use "I am" statements.

Chapter Eight: Bullet Journal

Go Deep with 5 Questions:

With your five questions, understand the values that you have written at the start of this chapter. Use these questions to learn in life. The first five questions I created for myself are:

1. Start with your WHY?
2. What did I learn today?
3. Who did I talk to?
4. What am I excited about?
5. How did I love myself today?

Every day for a week I asked myself these five questions. You are always learning and growing. These questions should change every day. Later on, I switched the questions to:

1. What gave me pleasure today?
2. What did I do to get clients today?
3. What am I excited about?
4. What did I learn today?
5. How did I love myself today?

Life is about growth. Life is about challenges and self-mastery. I love to ask questions. Give yourself permission to ask questions. I started a webinar on YouTube this year specifically to give people a platform where they could safely ask questions and learn. I believe growth is happiness. I believe growth is extremely uncomfortable but the only way to live to your unlimited potential.

Chapter Eight: Bullet Journal

The last concept for a bullet journal is thirty days to learn and dwell on a concept. I have a hard time with the concept of Pleasure, Grace, and Glory. So, I wrote at the top of a page:

"30 Days of Pleasure, Grace, and Glory"

… and filled in the blanks…

1. My company solves the pain problem of unemployment by teaching people the theory of how to get their dream career
2. Eye candy: A hot body!
3. Power moments: Launch a website, first client, the thought of opening my own company
4. Paying clients: people that see your value
5. The mountain moments: enjoying blessings
6. Excited expectations, pure pleasure: the buildup for fun
7. The early morning rise
8. Living outside the box and making your own rules
9. God being God
10. Peace: the feeling!
11. Performances: acting! Playing with passion
12. Marketing done right!
13. Slaying Dragons: The story – creative imagination
14. Feelings
15. Music
16. Sex, a good story, a good epiphany!
17. Figuring stuff out: wisdom

18. Working in your dream job
19. Rest
20. Excited expectations
21. Work out a problem I have been stuck on for a while
22. Sewing
23. Running in the rain
24. Girl's weekend
25. Music/Listening
26. Everything
27. Life
28. Wisdom
29. Friendship
30. Women: the seed within

Next thirty days: LOVE... I have no idea what love means. WHAT IS LOVE? I dwelled on the concept of love for a whole month this was the outcome of that month:

Thirty Days of LOVE

1. Work
2. Creative imagination
3. Argos and Azazel
4. Family
5. Friends
6. The rain

Chapter Eight: Bullet Journal

7. The mind and the possibilities I can create
8. Gorilla marketing
9. Being creative
10. Creative imagination: Yeah, I said it earlier, but I really love it!
11. Style, fashion, urban, skater
12. Converse/D.C.
13. Integrity
14. Authentic
15. Trust
16. Eating healthy
17. SURRENDER: letting go!
18. Clear communication
19. Learning
20. Being recognized for my work financially
21. Abundance
22. The Healing Journey
23. Growth
24. Leveling up!
25. Scheduling
26. Organizing
27. Closing the deal
28. Self
29. Magic

30. Coffee

From this Conceptual Journey, I learned about the seven types of love.

Different types of LOVE:

1. Romantic
2. Intimate
3. Playing
4. Unconditional
5. Self-Love
6. Committed, Compassion, Love
7. Empathy, Universal Love

Love is confusing but I think I have a better understanding of it from doing the fill-in-the-blank on "what does love mean for me" for thirty days. My favorite thirty days of learning a concept was "beauty." I live in boy land. I have a hard time thinking things are pretty, and for a woman that's weird. So...I thought I would sit in it. I would sit in the concept of thirty days of beauty; this was the outcome of it.

Thirty Days of Beauty

1. Guitar
2. Text and language
3. Define Terms of Beauty: "the combination of qualities such as shape, color, or form that pleases the aesthetic sense, especially the sigh."
4. A movie, a story, creative imagination
5. Music

Chapter Eight: Bullet Journal

6. The power of a network: people
7. Me
8. Pain and sadness (this one surprised me! I have found beauty in sadness)
9. Little children
10. The sun
11. The quiet hours of the morning
12. The heartbeat; the inner workings of the heart
13. Mental health and safety
14. Animals and nature
15. Spoken language
16. Rain
17. Artwork
18. Meeting new people: synergy
19. Feelings
20. Men manning UP! LOL
21. Trusting and laying your burdens down
22. SEX
23. The Beauty of a woman; raw POWER
24. The journey, the race
25. Being healthy
26. Understanding childhood trauma—facing it and releasing it
27. Sleep and naps

28. Grace

29. Wisdom

30. Showing up in life!

Life is about streams of living waters and streams of income. The only stability in life is the one we create. Find how to make money in seven different ways. Find a higher purpose, meditate, network, sing, read, learn, grow, and be uncomfortable. This book is a stream of income. I challenge you the reader to write your own book. If you start using bullet journals, meditate, do gratitudes, do goal setting, set intentions every morning, work on blessings, journal about the best part of your day, and visualize the future, you will have lots to write. Lastly, be blessed; enjoy the journey of your epic proportions.

Chapter Nine: A Little Crazy to Be an Entrepreneur

To: The Qualities of Entrepreneurship...

1. Broken: We see a problem and want to solve it the correct way.
2. Learning: We are open to figuring out life in a new way.
3. Hard Working: No, but really hard working. They spend 24/7 at the beginning thinking about their business and how to help people. (I totally get why most fail within the first year.)
4. Servant Hearts: This is one of my favorites. The number of cool entrepreneurs (I feel I always spell "entrepreneur" wrong) I have met because they generally care is mind-blowing.
5. Authentic: Every entrepreneur I have met. This is a pet peeve and a staple in the way they do business. Successful people are authentic.
6. Tenacious: Man, can they handle rejection.
7. Fun: They know how to play the game of life with excitement and entertainment. They do uncomfortable things on the regular.
8. Growing: They are pushing themselves to break pattern beliefs and become a new creation, something better—perhaps a Phoenix.
9. Healthy: Sort of! They are trying to live their best lives. They understand diet and exercise. Diet comes before exercise.

Chapter Nine: A Little Crazy to Be an Entrepreneur

10. They have mantras: I am hungry for knowledge. I have a mindset that is highly effective. I live in abundance.

11. They play with gratitudes every day.

12. They are magic.

Mike Oleskiw from CVL Engineers Inc. (Entrepreneur | Engineer | Ever Day Normal Guy) added two more to my list in a LinkedIn post one day. They will be added here as well...

13. Crazy: Slightly delusional, possibly a few screws loose.

14. Confident: Because who else would put themselves out there and risk so much if they weren't?

This is my favorite post from the first year of opening Phoenix Career Development.

Let's begin with an allegory: The dragons ate me! The dragons of self-hate, boredom, and control

What does a Legendary Journey look like?

Define Terms of Legendary: "remarkable enough to be famous, very well known." When did we give permission to shrink in life?

The process of life is meant to be enjoyed, but how do we enjoy life when second by second and day by day, life itself causes problems?

The simple answer is that we just choose to be. The complex answer is that we surrender and let it be. Life is about little disciples along the way; little wins and little goals to cross off a list and start over. It's about peace and meditation and being intentional about what we create in this moment and this time.

Chapter Nine: A Little Crazy to Be an Entrepreneur

The pet peeve in life is when people ask, "How is your day?" and people respond with, "Good," "Bad," or "O.K." Why do we sum up our day in those three categories? I am tired of living in mundane and boring.

=The Story of the Phoenix=

Life was mundane and boring. Alarm rings—wake up, brush teeth, get dressed, go to work, go home, watch T.V., have supper, watch more T.V., go to bed. Do it over and over and over again. Die with mundane and boring.

Self-hate speaks to you. Mundane and boring. Vapid existence in life, no goals, no hope, no motivation, death within life.

The fire comes. It burns, it burns so aggressively we change; we die. Our pattern beliefs get shaken to the core.

New creation forms—raw, authentic, beautiful. We transform into…what? What do you want to create?

www.phoenixcareerdevelopment.com

When people ask me how my day was, I respond with "Legendary." When people ask me, "How do you feel?" my response is, "Delightfully optimistic." Let the lion roar in your soul. You are allowed to be different. You are allowed to be weird. No one is like you. You are magnificent beauty. A little crazy to be an entrepreneur is the mindset behind running a successful empire. Define terms of success.

The Definition of Success by the Dalai Lama:

- The true hero is one who conquers his own anger and hatred.

- An open heart is an open mind.

- The roots of goodness lie in the soil of appreciation.

- The goal is not to be better than the other man, but your previous self.

Chapter Nine: A Little Crazy to Be an Entrepreneur

- A loving atmosphere in your home is the foundation for your life.

- Judge your success by what you had to give up in order to get it!

- Open your arms to change, but do not let go of your values.

- Share your knowledge. It's a way to achieve immortality.

It took me ten years to be an employment specialist. Once I believed in myself, it took two and a half months. The beast within is a real factor in being successful in business. The only way to get out of the rut of self-hate is to be a little crazy. My first year in the industry, one of my really good friends Sadia Awad said to me, "Hey, when you open your own company, I am going to work for you." I was shocked. I had never talked about running my own company or even thought about it.

The second job in my field came to me so naturally. Less than two weeks, and I knew everything I needed to do in order to help people with disabilities to clarify their career journeys. The third job in my field, I was tired of contract work. The thought of running my own company seemed to be something I was toying with for three years in the industry. One of my top values in life is stability. Control is an illusion; stability is something you create. I wanted to create stability in my life but had no idea how to do it. When I went to Anderson Career Training Institute, I knew the only thing stopping me from running a company was myself.

In order to run a successful company, you have to believe in yourself. You must believe in your narrative. You must step into the grace and glory you were created to achieve. I have always been a little crazy. The adventure of running an empire seemed as if, as Marianne Williamson stated, "Our deepest fear is that we are powerful beyond all measure." I wanted to step into the power of creative imagination. Life really is a journey of epic proportions. Life really is where your potential thrives. It's not about winning the race—it's about thriving in the beginning, middle, and end of the race.

Be blessed today and at this moment, stay epic.

Chapter Ten: The Last Chapter – Growth Is Uncomfortable

Being crazy is not the last chapter; growth is the last chapter. At Phoenix Career Development we believe growth is happiness. I failed grade 1. I can tell you the exact moment I failed. I was sitting at my desk reading a Peanuts book by Charles M. Schultz and could not understand what I was reading. In journal time we needed to write about what we read. I could not write. It was too hard and too painful. I sat there and created a pattern belief to give up, don't try, stop, fail. The internal turmoil within spoke like a dragon.

Growth and learning have always been difficult for me—tenaciously difficult. In fact, feeling dumb and being dumb is one of my biggest fears in life. I created comfortability. How do we drink from the wellspring of life? Every day we can create a life of death or a life of, well... living abundantly. Today is the day the best possible case scenario can come in.

The death moment in my life was sweet peace. It was complete healing. It was quiet. No one tells you a phoenix moment is quiet and no one around you sees it. You feel it by yourself. The fire is so intense you just put one foot in front of the other to burn and change.

The phoenix is spiritual. It usually has no words. Phoenix Career Development was birthed from self-love. My first year of being an entrepreneur can only be put into the concept of "In order to thrive in my life, I had to believe I could do it." This has been a year of new concepts— abundance, success, joy, grace, glory, and gratitude.

So many parables speak to us when we are younger. We eat baby food, and when we are older we need solid food to thrive. We as humans are hungry for knowledge. When we are stagnant in life, we die a spiritual death.

Chapter Ten: The Last Chapter – Growth Is Uncomfortable

Spiritual life is a concept where we as whole-body creatures are drinking from the living water. We are not deceived. Our wounds can come to a place of gratitude and can plug us into servant hearts, to heal people that are dying from living unfulfilled lives. The cross I picked up in life was, as I remember, the struggle of finding my purpose, mission, and vision. It is my responsibility to help people clarify their values in life and take their journey of epic proportions.

I do not fix people—I encourage, support, and inspire. My only responsibility in Phoenix Career Development is to create a program where your growth can be your happiness. Honestly, it does not make it easy. Growth is extremely uncomfortable. But the other option is stagnation and death.

Round two of grade 1 was an extreme blessing. I always thought it made me weak and stupid. I have come to a place in my life that failing grade 1 and taking it again laid the groundwork for becoming a pioneer in my industry. Perception makes a big difference. How we see the world, create the life that we live... once again, we can be better or bitter.

Take the journey of knowledge. Take the motif that in order to create a life where we drink from the living water, we must break.

I write this in heart pain—squeezing, twisting, grabbing, stabbing. My self-hate has left a mark on my soul. At this moment it feels like someone took out a large sharp sword from my heart and the raw emotions of unhappiness and failure feel like a stark reality in my life. I have created so much pain in my own life. I just want healing.

The Dragon Healing Meditation

Narrator: "Out of 10, how painful is your pain?" Me: "A solid 8."

Narrator: "Physically, with your hands, pull the pain out of your body. What does it look like? What does it look like? Play with your pain. Change your

Chapter Ten: The Last Chapter – Growth Is Uncomfortable

pain into a liquid, then into a solid. Look at your pain. Play with your pain. Change your pain into an animal."

Me (inner monologue): A big dragon; very beautiful, purple, black, and blue. Fiercely feminine. A part of me I never knew existed.

Narrator: "We sometimes need our pain to survive. We need our pain to make us feel alive. We are in control of our pain. We have created our pain for many reasons. Do you still want your pain? Does it serve you?"

Me (inner monologue): The pain in me. I am grateful for my pain because it helped me realize I was missing something in my life. I was missing growth and knowledge. My reaction: I want to change my pain to healing. I want to change my pain to little dragon babies—white, orange, yellow, and red. My result: I put the dragon babies of healing back into my heart.

Narrator: "What is your pain at now?" Me: "3."

In all my healing over the past three years of cardiomyopathy, my pain has always been an 8. This was the first time it was small, manageable, and tiny like a baby.

***   ***   ***   ***   ***   ***   ***   ***   ***

Complete healing is upon me. I slew the dragon of self-hate. I still have so many more pattern beliefs to shatter. I have so, so, so many lessons to learn and relearn again...argh. The empire is upon me. New creation is being formed. Growth is uncomfortable but it is the only way to have an abundant life and to build a highly successful mindset.

I have poured my soul into this book. I just hope you as the reader have been encouraged, supported, or blessed by me in a tiny way. You are the legend in your own life. You rescue yourself by surrendering to a higher

Chapter Ten: The Last Chapter – Growth Is Uncomfortable

purpose. It doesn't make sense. Growth is a journey; the best journey you can go on.

=PEACE=

Praise God, from whom all blessings flow. Praise him all creatures here below. Praise him above, ye heavenly hosts. Praise father, son, and Holy Ghost.

AMEN

A sneak peek of the second book in the series "A Journey of Epic Proportions"

The second book in the series is called
Round 2: DING, DING, DING! GRACE AND GLORY

Chapter 1: The Video Game

The second year in business includes the feeling of being overwhelmed and lets through twenty more missions in the game of life. The big bosses are not the enemy, they are networks that you align with.

Business has features, advantages, and benefits.

I don't want to create a life of being overwhelmed. How do we manipulate the game to win? Cheat codes, practice, and understand the theory behind it. Let's write a flawless script that will get to the point and start building relationships. Thank goodness the first year is over. To recap the first year in business—it was network, network, network.

Hello, my name is Laurette Lee, and I am the director of Phoenix Career Development. Round two in Business 2021 is that some people know me, like me, and trust me. Nuclear winter 2020 gave me a push up the hill just like Atlas in Greek mythology. This year, 2021, is forecasted to run down the hill. People know me, people like me, people trust me. People are starting to refer my services to others. Life is a slow play. We have to build a strong foundation in order to rise like a legend. Short cuts and shoddy workmanship don't result in quality every time.

Marketing Round Two includes the reps of the network, building relationships, round two, round three, round four and keep going until the Final Boss. Yes, we can find a warp tunnel and get ahead faster with synergy and wisdom. But at the end of the day, you still have to do the reps and put in the work.

Round Two in business includes Choose Your Own Adventure classes. That means creating all-new PowerPoints to back up my wisdom as an Employment Specialist so that others can teach my programming.

Classes like...Goal setting, The Phoenix Moments, Conflict in the Workplace: Project Management 101, Don't Sell yourself Short, Mindset, Star Technique, Manifestations and Storyboards, What Do You Want?, Fit for Life, Quick Fix, Career Development and the Entrepreneur, How to Cold Call, Interview Preparation, Transitions, and, last, Mission, Vision, and Purpose sessions.

And just like that, a pattern belief hits me... It knocks me down so hard I feel worthless. Define Terms: Worthlessness – "the state of being unimportant and useless."

The quiet moments are no longer peace. They gnaw at my soul. Little whispers scream at me with self-hate. A good distraction goes a long way and I try to fill myself with work, friends, and family. But at the end of the day, worthlessness wants to consume me! It wants to capture me and eat me up till I succumb to inferiority.

Round two in business is the fight for self-mastery. To win the game of business, unworthiness needs to be slain. I must step into my power of the Viking princess, understand my lineage, and claim my throne. The big boss in this video game is self; me feeling unworthy. The ticket to winning the game is self-mastery. How do we master ourselves?

First, understand why I feel unworthy. What is the pattern of belief behind my unworthiness? Sit in little girl Laurette. She is alone. She was alone in a family of six. I vied for attention. I screamed for it. I always wanted to be important, like my life mattered. The crippling fear of shyness and fighting for my parents' attention left me alone and feeling unworthy. This was my hello to unworthiness.

This was the rock in which I created my life of dream-killing. O.K., I faced my demon, and I understood it.

How do I create worthiness in my life? How do I create self-mastery? I wish I could have a quick fix. I wish I had the magic potion I could drink to become the victorious warrior. NOPE! No quick fix here. It's hard work. It's checks and balances. It's in process. "Come on a journey. Your Career Development Journey. Choose your own Adventure."

This is marketing 101 in my company. We believe in growth being uncomfortable. We believe you choose your own adventure. This is my adventure: Unworthiness to complete, whole, dignity, excellence, integrity, value, virtue, and worthiness. I am creating the Legendary Laurette by kicking unworthiness in the throat and stepping into self-mastery.

Define Terms: Self Mastery: (a Google definition) "the ability to control one's own desires or impulses; self-control, self-discipline." However, I realized that the wisdom of rookie advice and going away by myself to get over my anger requires my self-mastery.

My Definition: Self-Mastery is quiet; no one sees it. It's internal work. You see the spark afterward. It's a personal growth within. It's the growth in gross moments. It's the break, fire, and the Phoenix. Self-mastery is a routine for loving yourself. Love your growth, love your dark, light, and in between! Self-mastery is whole-body healing: heart, body, soul, and spirit. Self-mastery is the Legendary Journey.

What are we creating this year? What are we learning? Why is this year, Round Two, ding, ding, ding?

I don't believe in creating a fight. The second year is not about the fight. It's about the surrender of the punch. The surrender of the knockdown: pivot, pivot, pivot. Round Two ding, ding, ding is about getting back in the game. Do not quit. Every month we learn about different concepts. January and July concepts are Gratefulness and Fulfillment, February and August are the concept of abundance, March and September are Joy, April and October are How do you cultivate and develop your soul? and, lastly, June and December are Humor and Playfulness. These are the top values of what I am manifesting in my life. The epic journey is not done until we are dead. This day I get to live, I get to learn, I get to step into my power.

What does it mean to step into my power? I heard a rumor that when we love ourselves, we master ourselves, we become heirs to the throne of life. What does it mean to treat myself like a high priestess? Especially when most of my life I have lived in between being a magician and a fool?

What does power look like? Noun: "the ability to do something or act in a particular way or the capacity or ability to direct or influence the behavior of the course of events." When I walk into a room, people notice. When you are in a room, the energy shifts. That's power! I love wielding the power of creativity. It's my superpower. Green Lantern is my favorite superhero and I believe I am Green Lantern. In the video game of life, I am always Green Lantern.

Last year I gave up everything to be an entrepreneur and lost a 7-year relationship because starting a business is all-consuming. You breathe, eat, sleep, think, and walk audaciously through life. Your business is your baby, and you will die for it. Communication skills, learning a new language, and creating your game in life causes other people to face their demons and, well... we split the dogs. I got Argos; he got Azazel. I miss my healing puppy, but she was designed to love my ex when I couldn't; she molded into him. I know she loves me deeply, but she does not belong to me anymore. My puppy was sacrificed for my freedom to create an empire. A little oops along the way.

We got back together for a month after being away from each other for seven months. He made me the enemy. He was so mad at me...and then he broke. He crumbled and cried and fell in love with me again. I will always love my ex. A special place resides in my heart for him. While I was with him, my company could not attract clients. He became indecisive and demanded to know how much Phoenix Career Development made in its first year of being open. He wanted to control my marketing. He told me my cyndicate and the dream team are cults and not to trust others.

He doesn't know I am part of a powerful force of titan. He doesn't know how strong a tribe is. I am in too deep with self-mastery for his game to work. Our first breakup was lightning, a tower moment of loud shouts and disagreements all over the place. The last and second breakup ended with a silent tear.

Ex: "Your hippy legendary marketing is stupid."

Me: (with a single tear) "I believe in myself; I believe in the legendary journey. I believe in the dream career."

Phone call over. Peace and absolute singleness. I believe in myself wholeheartedly. I believe I can create stability in my own life. When most women break up with men, they become the victim. I thrived in a break-up. Yes, I throw myself into work. I find meaning, purpose, and mission in work. I am a workaholic; that's why this year, Round Two, is self-mastery, video games, and evil bosses, grace, and glory.

I have things to do and people to see. Direct marketing is coming. Private B.C. Schools and Saskatchewan educational institutions are going to be my best friends. The game of life is better than a video game. Let's go make some friends...

Let's level up. Instead of a Director, I gave myself a new title in my business. I have become the CEO, OOOOOOOH of Phoenix Career Development.

www.ingramcontent.com/pod-product-compliance
Lightning Source LLC
Chambersburg PA
CBHW062035120526
44592CB00036B/2134